Faithbook

A guide to sharing your faith with other faiths

Faithbook

A guide to sharing your faith with other faiths

MARK GREENWOOD

Copyright © Mark Greenwood 2014

First published in 2014. Revised edition published in 2021.

revmarkgreenwood.com

revmarkgreenwood@gmail.com

Published for Mark Greenwood

by Verité CM Limited

Worthing, BN12 4BG, UK

veritecm.com

The right of Mark Greenwood to be identified as the author of this work
has been asserted by him in accordance with the Copyright, Designs and
Patents Act 1988.

ISBN No. 978-1-914388-16-3

British Library Cataloguing Data

A catalogue record of this book is available from The British Library.

Scripture quotations are taken from The Holy Bible, New International
Version (Anglicised edition), copyright © 1979, 1984, 2011 by Biblica. Used by
permission of Hodder & Stoughton Publishers, an Hachette UK company.

All rights reserved.

Printed in England

Designed by Ashdown Creative

CONTENTS

INTRODUCTION
Please do read!

Dear Reader

Welcome to this handy guide to sharing your faith with other faiths – it's a guide and by no means exhaustive.

I'm not an expert at sharing my faith in any particular faith group but, as an evangelist, I've been travelling the UK since 1988, during which time I've chatted with people from all the groups mentioned in chapter 3. I've also spent many hours with friends who have a different faith from me – I reflect that experience in this booklet.

I put this book together primarily for my own use as I find that I can quickly forget the information if I don't use it. I then realised it would be a useful tool for many people – I pray you find it informative and practical. My aim isn't to give you an in-depth analysis and study of any particular faith but rather to give you an overall equipping to share with lots of different faiths. If you feel more drawn or called to sharing amongst a particular faith, or if you find you are talking more to a person from a particular faith, I would encourage you to get a greater understanding of that particular group. I did this with a Jehovah's Witness and found it invaluable. It gave me a real confidence when I got into conversation.

I lived in Bradford till the age of twenty-five and regularly found myself in conversation with Muslims and Jehovah's Witnesses. As I did this I wanted to understand their religion and be as effective as I could be in sharing with them; this changed the way I viewed them. I began to see them as people who genuinely wanted to connect with God but sadly had been misinformed and misled. Let me encourage you to view them the same – I believe you will have a healthier time with them. I would encourage you to be prepared to spend some good quality time with the people you share with and you will see in most cases their desire for God. You'll need to be patient and loving and not expect to see change overnight.

May I recommend you do some more learning about how you can share your faith more effectively with people in general. I've recorded my four-week personal evangelism course called *The Boot Camp* and it is available for you to buy through our website www.revmarkgreeenwood.com. You will find the course in our shop along with lots of other great resources.

I would just say three more things in conclusion:

1.   Let's remember it's God who convicts people of their need of him – our responsibility is simply to share the gospel with people in a way that is clear and sensitive. I have included some testimonies of people who have converted to Christ from another faith.

2.   I really believe in giving people things they can take away, so make sure you have lots of resources to leave with people. Visit my website for some resources www.revmarkgreenwood.com.

3.   Make all your evangelism natural – best to share within the context of friendship that is genuine. As the saying goes – 'keep it real'.

Let me leave you with this verse:

> *We are therefore Christ's ambassadors, as though God were making his appeal through us.* (2 Corinthians 5:20)

Let's be great ambassadors for our God.

Hope you enjoy reading.

Mark

Mark Greenwood

1
They aren't the enemy!

I wonder how you view people from another faith or a cult. We do often see them in an unhelpful way whilst also being a bit ignorant of their beliefs and practices. We can end up seeing them as 'the enemy' and yet in truth the vast majority of them are people with a genuine desire to connect with God – something I believe God has put in each one of us.

If I am really honest, that used to be my attitude. Whether it was a conversation that just happened, or one that had been planned, my mindset was very much to win against the person. I am not proud of that but that was my plan. It came from good intentions – to get the person to see the error of their religion – but it wasn't a good approach as you become more focused on proving your point rather than sensitively guiding the person. I have to watch my argumentative side!

Let's remind ourselves of this: 'For our struggle is not against flesh and blood, but against the rulers, against the authorities, against the powers of this dark world and against the spiritual forces of evil in the heavenly realms' (Ephesians 6:12). With any evangelism we need to go to war with the real enemy and this is never more true than with someone who has been deceived in their search for God. Fight the enemy and lovingly journey with the person.

I believe these days that all evangelism is most fruitful within the context of relationship and understanding – both grow at the same rate! If I look at our world we have so many problems due to a lack of relationship and understanding. If only we would seek to understand each other we would walk together better. I once heard said, 'We may not see eye to eye, but we can walk arm in arm.' We mustn't sell out on what we stand for but we must build relationally with people from other faiths, seeking to understand them as we share our faith with them and they share theirs with us. This I have found is the best approach.

Whilst I totally believe Jesus is the only way to God and a true connection with him, it's my experience that people in other faiths and belief systems do feel some sense of spiritual fulfilment. We may think about them simply living up to rules and regulations, but actually they see it as a way of life that often affects their culture and the decisions they make.

Let me also say at this point that in some of the more extreme cults or sects there is also a fear in the followers, that if they left there would be consequences. We must be aware that asking a person to follow Christ is a bigger decision than we realise; never is this more true than with people from other faiths. We are asking them to give up more than most of us gave up when we chose to follow Christ. Against that backdrop let's develop real relationship and understanding.

I'm very fond of 1 Peter 3:15 which encourages us to 'always be prepared to give an answer to everyone' but it also encourages us to do this with 'gentleness and respect'. I would like to treat both aspects of this verse with equal importance.

We have often focused on the readiness aspect of that verse from 1 Peter – which clearly we must be – but let's have a complete understanding and be as much committed to being 'always prepared' as we are to being gentle and respectful. Going in tough isn't always the best approach!

Colossians 4:5-6 says, 'Be wise in the way you act towards outsiders; make the most of every opportunity. Let your conversation be always full of grace, seasoned with salt, so that you may know how to answer everyone.'

Again we can often focus on the 'make the most of every opportunity' and forget the 'let your conversation be always full of grace, seasoned with salt, so that you may know how to answer everyone'.

I think this is a great verse in the Bible that's a good principle for any kind of sharing of our faith – it's particularly appropriate for when we share our faith with other faiths. If we aren't careful we can find our words aren't full of grace. If we attack what is personal to them we will find fewer opportunities to discuss, not more. Why not find out what you can agree on before you get to what you disagree on. Maybe then the strength of our relationship may be a better place to share from.

Let me also say at this point that 'make the most of every opportunity' doesn't necessarily mean 'get as much of the gospel across as possible'. I often talk about actively creating journey in our evangelism. What I mean by this is: seeking to say as much as we can doesn't always mean we have been understood as much as we could be or that the person hearing has heard as they should. This is why I believe faith sharing is best done in relationship over time. Here are a few things that will prepare us well as we get better at sharing our faith with other faiths.

First things first

With any opportunity we get to share our faith with someone of another faith, the temptation is that we hog the limelight. How about before you share yours you get them to share theirs?

Whenever I get to know anyone who has a strong belief in another faith, religion or cult, this is what I say to them: 'Hey [their name], I would love to have a chat and find out why you are a [whatever faith] and the difference it makes in your life and I would love to share with you why I am a Christian and the difference it's made in my life. I won't try to convert you and you won't try to convert me.' I find this approach works well.

In the same way that Christianity has a breadth of beliefs and cultures it is true of many (not all) cults and religions that there is variance. This would be more the case for the main religions in the world and less true of the cults. All that said, when I have built relationally with people from cults so they trust me, I have discovered that they don't always personally hold one hundred per cent to what is organisational doctrine or beliefs. They would hold the organisational belief publicly due to fear, but inwardly they are processing it differently. This is why often people convert. Let's understand that whether an atheist, Muslim or a Jehovah's Witness, there's nearly always a journey that involves starting to doubt about their own conviction as they journey towards Christ.

Again let me emphasise the importance of journeying with someone, building friendship and getting to know and understand them. You will in this process see where they are and where they may have a 'tugging' away from their belief towards Christ and the uniqueness of who he is and what he offers.

Get to know the other faiths

We have chatted about getting to know the person in the faith and now we are going to think about the faith in the person. I'll say a bit more about this in chapter 3 but just at this point I would like to encourage you to get to know the types of questions that you are going to be asked by people from other faiths. This isn't so that you can gain 'one-upmanship' but rather that you can give thought-through answers to the questions you are asked. I found this prevented me from being off guard and so better enabled me to be gentle in my response. This will show that you are more serious about your own faith.

You can't do this with every faith but it might be a good idea to recognise which faiths you are more likely to be in relationship with, or have conversation with, and spend some time researching them. This may well be an 'in the moment thing'. For example, if you find yourself around Muslims a lot, it would be wise to get to know their faith. If at another time you find yourself around Jehovah's Witnesses, spend some time getting to know what their history and beliefs are. I have certainly done this throughout my life and I have found it stands me in good stead and stops me stereotyping and misunderstanding. I think also it shows to the person that you are more informed about their faith and, let's face it, we all prefer it when we are not misunderstood.

Keep meeting with them

As we've discussed, with any conversion it's a process and as with all people we share our faith with, you will need to help them along that journey. When a person from another belief system becomes a Christian it is a massive commitment and they will feel very vulnerable – not least by facing the possibility they may be ostracised from even their own family. It's crucial, therefore, to introduce them to lots of Christians who will encourage them in their faith as well as you meeting them. This is also true at the point when they begin to doubt what they have believed for many years. Let's not underestimate the choice they face. We are asking them to change their identity!

I think sharing faith is best done in community and so don't underestimate the power of introducing people to your Christian friends. It's also true to say they will meet them before they will come to church with you. It's a safer environment for them in terms of how they will be viewed by their faith community if they found out they'd been to a church.

In the next chapter we will look at what it means to be a good ambassador for our faith to other faiths. But first be encouraged as you read Sandy Monro's story.

From Mormonism to Christ
SANDY'S STORY

Growing up I always had a belief in God even though my parents had no faith. When I was about twelve all my friends were being confirmed in the Church of England so I asked my parents if I could be confirmed too. They replied that I hadn't been baptised as they wanted me to make my own decision when I was old enough. I thought deeply about this and started 'window shopping' for a church. I was a crazy fan of the Osmonds so, along with my cousin, we started attending the local Mormon church and it wasn't long before I wanted to be baptised. My parents initially told me I was too young at fourteen to make my own decision but eventually I wore them down. I was baptised but they did not support me in this.

I was very involved right from the beginning. I attended the youth programme and the four-year study of Mormon scriptures. Marriage and family are emphasised in Mormon life so I got engaged to a Mormon man when I was nineteen. I had a bad feeling about it and broke off our engagement and then decided to go on a mission instead. Mormon boys are strongly encouraged to go, girls less so. My parents were horrified at the thought of me going away for eighteen months with no telephone contact with them, only a weekly letter. I was so sucked in at that point that I really didn't consider their feelings – something I deeply regret now. To make matters worse, I left five days before Christmas to serve in the Belgium mission. It was on my mission that I started to have doubts about the church but I was too embarrassed to admit defeat to anyone. I didn't want to come home dishonourably so I stayed on and came back to a hero's welcome.

I had no idea what to do for a job when I got back so I was delighted to learn that there was a vacancy for a secretary in the London Temple. Although I enjoyed my work, I soon realised the mistake I had made. I was living in church accommodation (in the middle of nowhere) and my job, my friends, my social life were all tied up in the church. I was trapped. I was deeply unhappy.

After two years, my mum started to develop symptoms of what we later found out was multiple sclerosis. I attended a lot of hospital appointments with her and this sparked my interest in becoming a nurse. I left my job at the Temple and moved just a few miles away to do my nurse training. As this involved working different shifts, I found I was attending church less and less. At first this bothered me but it gradually became less important to me.

I was drifting away from the Mormon church but there was no one thing that made me leave. This was pre-internet days, so the church history wasn't readily available. I hadn't fallen out with anyone, committed any major sin or lost my faith in any way. I probably would've continued as I was but during this time I wrote a letter to a Mormon 'friend of a friend'. I expressed my view that there is too much emphasis on the Book of Mormon and not enough on the Bible. That was all. I was completely amazed to receive a badly typed letter from the bishop a few weeks later saying he had been instructed by the First Presidency of the church to remove my name from the membership roll! I had two weeks to appeal. By this stage I already felt I had left, so I didn't take any action. Looking back, I feel it would've been nice to speak to someone face to face and have a proper conversation, but I don't regret being excommunicated.

I was upset for a while but knew that there was still a God-shaped hole in my life so I started 'window shopping' for a church again, just like my fourteen-year-old self. This time I got it right! I walked into a small Baptist church and started theological arguments with the long-suffering pastor, claiming I was already a Christian. He patiently spent hours telling me about the real Christian faith and answering my questions.

Eventually he gave me a small pamphlet called *Just Grace*. I argued that it couldn't be that simple. What about works? What about keeping all the commandments? What about being worthy? All my Mormon thinking was blown away by this simple truth that Jesus had died to pay for my sins. I was baptised as a Christian believer and knew that I had made the right decision.

Shortly after I got married (to a wonderful Christian man I met at the Baptist church), the London Temple was open to the public prior to it being re-dedicated. We went on the tour together and I remember feeling very embarrassed that I had ever believed in it all. For a long time, I would leave out the Mormon part of my life story. I felt that sometimes people ask 'What's the difference between Christians and Mormons?' and I only wanted to tell them about the real Jesus. However, I have now been a Christian for over thirty years and I have recently become a member of several groups on social media witnessing to Mormons.

It took a number of years to finally get rid of all the Mormon theology as it was so engrained in me. For someone who has never been in a cult, Mormon or other, it can be really hard to understand how people get involved and how they stay. My answer would be that it becomes your whole life; you see it as normal and everyone else is wrong! From my personal experience it's no use trying to argue theology, just be gentle and show the love of Jesus to them. Jesus' grace is all they need to know.

Know your own faith

Let me encourage you to know your own faith – what you believe and why you believe it. Know your own Holy Book, read it cover to cover and memorise the Scriptures. Look into all the difficult areas that other faiths may pick up on and make sure you have a well-thought-through answer.

Whilst it's not about winning the argument, if we are weak in knowledge about our own faith when we chat to people of other faiths, what does that say to them? It says that we don't take it very seriously and so shouldn't be listened to. If we can give strong and robust answers to their questions it will stand us in good stead – this can really create a respect for us as they see us as a genuine Christian.

I run a course on sharing your faith and during that I teach what the gospel is. I teach five key points:

- God's plan

- Our problem

- Our effort

- God's solution

- Our response

I set a challenge for the delegates to give me a Bible verse for each point including full text and full reference. Very rarely (in fact three times in twenty years) has someone been able to give me five – I've done this quite literally with thousands of people. Most can only give one verse and that's normally John 3:16!

I have now recorded this course as *Boot Camp Lite* and it is available for anyone and any group to use completely free of charge. You can download it at: revmarkgreenwood.com/product/boot-camp-lite/

Celebrate your own faith

As well as considering how we share with other faiths I think we need to think about how we live out our faith. The truth is many Christians will be put to shame by how committed we are or aren't to our own faith. Not that this should be the motive per se but it is something worth bearing in mind. I know that many of the very committed people from other faiths do so because of fear and control, and so I am clearly not encouraging that. But what I am saying is that if we are serious about engaging with those from other faiths we ought to make sure we are worthy of the badge we wear.

I remember chatting to some Muslims and at that time I was in an extended time of prayer and fasting. They were seriously impressed and their level of respect for me increased as I was serious about my own faith. Be as intent to live out your own faith as you are to share with other faiths.

I think anyone who takes their faith seriously will earn respect from someone in another faith or cult. Don't be afraid – in fact I would argue it's a must – to talk about such things as your prayer life, how you read the Bible, and so on.

When we engage in conversation we're often found with a serious lack of knowledge about what we believe, and where in the Bible that verse is. I don't feel it's enough for us to know that it's two thirds of the way through and highlighted in orange! (By the way, a quick note on that: don't use your marked-up Bible when sharing with Muslims and don't put the Bible on the floor – this shows disrespect for your Holy Book.) We need to get to know our own Holy Book better. And by the way, there are a number of sections in the Bible that would be picked up on by cults and faiths which they will use to show that the Bible has been changed or contradicts, and so we would do well to read and study those and be able to answer any questions. This shows that our Holy Book is trustworthy and that we study it.

Know the gospel, share the gospel

You will find that there will be times when you move into sharing the whole gospel and not just debating the person and deity of Christ. It's really important to share the gospel with people from other faiths. All that said, if you start with sharing the gospel it may well be in the sharing of this that issues with regard to Jesus' identity and resurrection could be challenged. We will deal with that in chapter 4. We will look at sharing about Jesus' death at this point which is the real power to save anyone. Paul reminds us of this in Romans 1:16. So how do I share it? I generally do it using the following illustration.

Imagine, if you will, that you are out walking on a dark night and you fall down a very deep pothole breaking your arms and legs – you are unable to move. To make things worse, the water level is rising, giving you only a short time before you will be totally submerged. You start to shout for help as you are totally unable to do anything to get yourself out.

Someone walks along and hears your shouts. They look down and say, 'I can see you are in trouble and unable to get out so what you need to do is . . .' They begin to tell you lots of stuff that all depends on you getting yourself out. That person then walks away. Your shouts continue until another person comes by and says, 'I can see you are in trouble so you need to enter into a state of inner peace and deny and ignore the trouble you are in.' They then continue on their way.

I use this talk to illustrate the fact that there is nothing we can do to get ourselves out of the mess we are in. There's nothing we can do to forget or ignore the reality or escape it. What we need is someone who will rescue us.

At this point, as you're shouting, another person walks by, looks down the pothole and says, 'I can see you are in trouble and that there is nothing you can do so I will come down and get you out myself.' That's the kind of help you want! I talk about how the mess we are in is a result of our wrongdoing and only Jesus can rescue us.

I share John 14:6 in which Jesus says, 'I am the way and the truth and the life. No one comes to the Father except through me.' The significance of Jesus saying this is that he is the only one who has come from heaven to earth and then gone back. I'm more likely to trust Jesus because he's done the journey. I do this because, as you will see later in this book, being able to share well about Jesus is key to giving you a general guide to sharing your faith with other faiths.

I learned this amazing truth about what Jesus fully meant when he said, 'I am the way.' If you asked a Jewish person for directions in Bible times they wouldn't give you a set of directions and then let you try to remember them as you make your way, hoping to follow them correctly. They would say, 'I am the way,' and with that would grab a hold of your hand and they wouldn't let go until they got you to the place you were looking for. When Jesus said, 'I am the way,' he was saying, 'Observe this, do that, don't do that . . .' What he was saying was that if you grab a hold of his hand he will get you to the Father and to heaven. Now at the risk of a mini-preach here, how good is that? This makes more sense of that whole part of John.

Do not let your hearts be troubled. You believe in God; believe also in me. My Father's house has many rooms; if that were not so, would I have told you that I am going there to prepare a place for you? And if I go and prepare a place for you, I will come back and take you to be with me that you also may be where I am. You know the way to the place where I am going.' Thomas said to him, 'Lord, we don't know where you are going, so how can we know the way?' Jesus answered, 'I am the way and the truth and the life. No one comes to the Father except through me. (John 14:1-6)

I will more often than not use this story, verse and explanation as a springboard to sharing the gospel with people from other faiths. Of course it's Jesus who is the way and not the cross! I think it's really important to introduce people from other faiths to Jesus and not just his death. I will say more about how we can do this later in the book.

Here is my simple outline of the gospel with a verse. I encourage you to learn these as part of the getting to know your own Holy Book challenge.

1. God's Plan

'"For I know the plans I have for you," declares the LORD, "plans to prosper you and not to harm you, plans to give you hope and a future."' (Jeremiah 29:11)

2.   Our Problem

'We all, like sheep, have gone astray, each of us has turned to our own way; and the LORD has laid on him the iniquity of us all.' (Isaiah 53:6)

3.   Our Effort

'For it is by grace you have been saved, through faith – and this is not from yourselves, it is the gift of God – not by works, so that no one can boast.' (Ephesians 2:8-9)

4.   God's Solution

'Jesus answered, "I am the way and the truth and the life. No one comes to the Father except through me."' (John 14:6)

5.   Our Response

'Yet to all who did receive him, to those who believed in his name, he gave the right to become children of God.' (John 1:12)

I would encourage you to download the *Boot Camp Lite* sessions I mentioned to give you a fuller unpacking of how to communicate the gospel well.

Share your testimony

I really believe in the power of testimony and so make sure you share your own personal story. Talk about what your life was like before you became a Christian. If you don't remember a time when you weren't a Christian because you were brought up in a Christian family, then you can talk about the time when you made a more fully informed decision. Talk about how you became a Christian and why you did so. Talk about your journey with God since that time.

The important thing to emphasise is relationship with God through Jesus and what he did. It's not about how good we are but more about God's grace. Talk about things that you have prayed for and God has answered your prayers. Have you experienced something supernatural e.g. a healing or a provision that could only have been God? If you haven't you could share someone else's story alongside yours.

A simple framework you may already have used is based around sharing the three key stages of your journey:

1. Before conversion. What did you think about God and Christianity? What was your experience of religion? If you were brought up as Christian (i.e. you don't remember a time when you weren't a Christian) then make your 'Before Conversion' the time in your life before you made it your own personal faith, or when you had an experience that made it more real or when you made a more fully informed decision.

2. During conversion. What was it that made you commit to Christ? Here you can spend a little more time talking about Jesus and his death and how that made you feel.

3. After conversion. What's it been like since? What are the benefits of being a Christian? Include the assurance of salvation not based on anything you have done.

In all three areas make sure you tell the story of your life and make sure you don't *preach* your testimony. I would aim to have two versions: one you can tell in three minutes and one you can tell in six minutes. Of course you may not always get the time to do it this way but it's good to have it framed well so you can tell a more balanced testimony. Once again, let me encourage you to download my *Boot Camp Lite* sessions where there is one on telling your story.

Offer to pray for them

This isn't always acceptable but actually sometimes there is opportunity and it can be appreciated. Be sensitive – I've heard people praying and they have done it like the person is not in the room! I would tend to pray to God thanking him that he wants all people everywhere to know him. On the basis this is actually a verse from the Bible it's a great prayer. I would ask God to reveal himself to the person as they seek him. Thank God that you get to journey together to discover him.

As much as you are used to laying on hands in church when praying for people, it's not best practice when praying for people in a one-on-one context. Touch isn't something that everybody is comfortable with.

In the next chapter we will look at knowing who is around us and understanding their faiths. But first, be encouraged as you read Marisa's story.

From Wicca to Christ

MARISA'S STORY

A number who had practised sorcery brought their scrolls together and burned them publicly. (Acts 19:19)

The city of Ephesus, circa AD 52. The masses had brought their spell books, pagan instruments and artefacts to the city centre, the value burnt that day was estimated at 50,000 drachmas (millions in today's money). Turning to Christ and his message of hope, these people abandoned their idols. Lacking much of the drama, and monetary value, a similar fire took place in a non-descript Essex town in 2009. It poured that day. Thankfully, the fire didn't extinguish, and a small gathering of believers persevered in tipping bags of pagan content into the flames. Bemused neighbours observing the spectacle noticed a soaked twenty-year-old woman stood closest to the fire. A former witch, now a Christian, enthusiastically torching nine years of torment. Separated by centuries and geography, the Essex girl and the Ephesians had two things in common: fire and freedom.

The Essex region has a long association with witchcraft; infamous trials, numerous covens and folk stories, all were brought to my attention as I grew up. They resonated with me, but the first eleven years were only peppered with agnosticism. Whispers of old Jewish traditions, a dab of Catholic superstitions and hints of Protestant habits melded together in my diverse family. The most impactful element in late childhood, however, came in the hard-backed form of the Harry Potter book series. I was already watching various TV programmes about the craft but the singular impact these books had was immeasurable. Not being the happiest of children I was captured by these empowered characters, not dissimilar in age. If they could harness such power and control, why couldn't I? If magic helped them, protected them, made them brave, why wouldn't it with me?

In 2000 I set up a small altar in my bedroom. I was eleven years of age. The proceeding nine years spiralled into the depths. I incorporated all kinds of practices into the craft, adopting Far Eastern and New Age practices: meditation, reflexology, yoga, palm reading, tarot cards, the list goes on. Simultaneously, my mental health declined. Aged thirteen, desperate to become psychic, I induced myself into trances asking 'spirit guides' to possess and empower me. By fourteen I was an inch away from a complete breakdown. Hallucinations, voices, self-harming, delusions and paranoia led me to numerous specialists, therapies and medication. Nothing worked. My formative years were a cycle of deepening craft practices and spiralling mental health. Nothing was working, the despair was all consuming. Twice I attempted to take my own life, I couldn't even get that right. But God had a plan.

I was eighteen and despite my insecurities and instability I was accepted into university in 2006. Heavily medicated, reclusive, but armed with my books, I moved into Halls. It was here that I came into regular contact with Christians, the ones calling themselves 'born again', whatever that meant. They were different. Really different. They exuded a peace and compassion I hadn't seen before; they were set apart. I had so many questions. It took three years, my entire university experience, of asking questions, attempting to read a Bible, trying to 'talk' to Jesus to find what it was that separated Christians from everyone else. Many spend far longer searching and questioning. In my final year I found 'it'; he had been in plain sight all along. Invited to church by housemates, I squirmed uncomfortably in the converted school hall. Hadn't the church brought misery and persecution to my community for millennia? What was a seasoned witch doing in a Sunday church service? But this peace was everywhere, there was joy and an enthusiasm for life. I had to keep coming back and know the answer.

It took some weeks, then one Sunday the pastor reiterated the gospel, the meaning of life. Everything fell into place. I had been trying to talk to this Christian God like I spoke to the lord and lady of the forest, but someone was missing – Christ. The mediator, the only way to the Father, the One who came to set me free. I didn't need convincing of my sin: I had an altar in my room, I had practised the dark arts for almost ten years, embraced all manner of destruction, I was a sinner. But God, he had made a way for reconciliation, a new start – Christ. All I had to do was accept his sacrifice on the cross, that one act of faith was going to wipe the stains away. I had felt filthy for so long, then I read, 'Wash me, and I shall be whiter than snow' (Psalm 51:7). This was the missing piece. That night I asked for forgiveness, that night I was made new.

Like the Ephesians, I now know redemption.

The years of darkness were not in vain. The Lord not only forgave and restored, he called me to the mission field in 2018. Now sharing the good news with pagans around the Amazon basin and the Andean regions, his mercy knows no bounds.

Therefore, if anyone is in Christ, the new creation has come: the old has gone, the new is here! (2 Corinthians 5:17)

3

Know who
is around

How well do you know the people around you?
Depending on where you live you will rub
shoulders with people on various levels from
various faiths. We need to understand that there
will be a whole breadth of commitment to the religion a
person 'subscribes to'. Just as with Christianity, there are
people who broadly sign up to the label without it actually
affecting their lifestyle. You may know, for example, people
who are affected by Buddhist teaching without classing
themselves as Buddhist. You may know some who call
themselves Muslim but don't go to mosque.

The other thing to consider is just as with people who used to be Christians but have slipped and people who have been brought up in Christian families but decided it wasn't for them, there are those who are in the same situation in other faiths, religions and cults. This may make them cynical of Christianity (and in fact any faith belief system) as they see them all in the 'same boat'. It can be really helpful in journeying with these people, too, if you know what their faith taught so you can distance Christianity from those. So it's not just for those who are committed to their faith that we need to learn more to better engage; it's for those who have been affected by them – often negatively – that this will really help.

Of course it would also be helpful on a broader evangelism front when we face the question: 'Aren't all faiths basically the same?' The implication here is that all faiths are fundamentally the same and superficially different. The truth is that all faiths are fundamentally different and superficially the same. The more we show that we have a good grasp of all these faiths, the better equipped we will be when answering this question. I am not suggesting that you do a degree in world religions and faiths but it would be good to get ourselves better acquainted. I have found knowing the principles we will look at in this book to be a very useful starting point – it has worked for me for over thirty years.

The main groups you are likely to come across are:

Buddhism, Christadelphian, Christian Science, Hare Krishna, Hinduism, Islam, Jehovah's Witnesses, Judaism, Mormons, New Age, Scientology, Sikhism, Spiritualism and Wicca/Paganism.

The faiths that are around are as varied in age as they are in beliefs. I want to encourage you to get to know as much as you can about the background of the faiths that surround you. The following table gives you the name of the founder. It's not always as easy to be specific about the date but wherever I can that's also included.

NAME	FOUNDER, MAIN WRITINGS AND PRACTICES
Buddhism	Gautama in around 510 BC. Theravada Buddhism has three main writings, Tripitaka, which are gathered oral traditions of more than 300 years. Mahayana Buddhism has over 5,000 holy writings. Buddhists need to keep moral laws and ceremonial observances.

NAME	FOUNDER, MAIN WRITINGS AND PRACTICES
Christadelphian	Dr John Thomas first published his teachings in England in 1848 but his school of thought originated in the USA in 1844. They use the King James Bible, Elpis Israel, Christendom Astray and other writings by John Thomas and Russell Roberts. A great emphasis is placed upon Israel in their teaching, and Bible exhibitions are regularly held.
Christian Science	Mary Baker Eddy after a 'miraculous' healing in 1866. First church was established in 1879. They use Science and Health with a key to the scriptures as well as Eddy's other writings. Healing is the central theme and they believe that sin, sickness and death are not real.

NAME	FOUNDER, MAIN WRITINGS AND PRACTICES
Hare Krishna	A.C. Bhaktivedanta Swami Prabhupada in 1969 but traced back to ancient Hinduism. They use eighteen chapters from Bhagavad-Gita from the Mahabharata and the Vedic scriptures which are the spiritual literature of the ancient Indian culture. It is essential to be vegetarian and to repeat a mantra many times throughout the day.
Hinduism	No one person but three main influences: Indo European, Iranian and Indian dating back to 1500 BC. They use the Mahabharata which contains the Bhagavad-Gita, Rigveda, Upanishads, Purana and many other texts. Yoga and meditation are central parts of the beliefs and practices for many Hindus.

NAME	FOUNDER, MAIN WRITINGS AND PRACTICES
Islam	Mohammed around AD 610. They use only the Qur'an (Koran). They have 'Five Pillars' of faith which are: daily recitation of the shahada (an Islamic oath), prayers five times a day, alms (giving), fasting during Ramadan and pilgrimage to Mecca.
Jehovah's Witnesses	Charles Taze Russell in 1870s. They use the New World translation of the Bible and anything published by the Watchtower Bible and Tract Society. They believe Jesus returned invisibly in 1914. They believe God bans blood transfusions and that celebrating Christmas, Easter and birthdays is pagan.

NAME	FOUNDER, MAIN WRITINGS AND PRACTICES
Judaism	The God of the Jews through the patriarchs. They use the Tanakh (Old Testament) and in particular the Torah (first five books), the Mishnah, Talmud and writings of Rabbis Rashi and Maimonides. They seek to keep the law of the Torah and celebrate a variety of biblical festivals and added traditions. Circumcision and Bar Mitzvah are important.
Mormons	Joseph Smith received the first visions in 1820. They use the Book of Mormon, Pearl of Great Price, Doctrine and Covenants, and the King James Bible. Importance of the family is a primary message. They have scared temple ceremonies with secret passwords and special handshakes.

NAME	FOUNDER, MAIN WRITINGS AND PRACTICES
New Age	No single founder. Beliefs date back to old ways of Paganism and Eastern mysticism sprinkled with Western humanism. Because New Age is an umbrella name, there are many different writings and scriptures used and in the main these are of Eastern influence. They are looking for the dawning of the Age of Aquarius and the New Earth.
Scientology	L. Ron Hubbard in 1951 although the very first church of scientology was founded in 1954, developed from a set of ideas that he called Dianetics, which is one of their writings, along with all other works by Hubbard.

NAME	FOUNDER, MAIN WRITINGS AND PRACTICES
Sikhism	Guru Nanak regarded as the founder (1469–1539) although Guru Gobind Singh (1666–1708) formalised their religion. They use the Adi Granth (First Scripture), more commonly called the Guru Granth Sahib. The second most important scripture of the Sikhs is the Dasam Granth. Both of these consist of text which was written or authorised by the Sikh Gurus. Sikhs are required to undertake the following observances: wake up very early in the morning; bathe and cleanse the body; cleanse the mind by meditating on God.
Spiritualism	Thought to be revived by the Fox sisters in 1848 but the roots are traced back much further. They use many occult writings (e.g. White Eagle) and some would even use the Bible! Most of the time is taken up with healing and developing the gifts of mediumship.

NAME	FOUNDER, MAIN WRITINGS AND PRACTICES
Wicca/Paganism	No single founder; civilisations such as ancient Saxon, Greek, Roman, Celtic and Norse have influenced. Many different writings are accepted as many different traditions come under the heading. They celebrate 'The Wheel of the Year', a symbol which represents the eight festivals important to many pagans, Wiccans and witches. These holidays – known as Sabbats – follow a nature-based calendar and include four solar festivals and four seasonal festivals set in between them.

NAME	WHAT THEY BELIEVE ABOUT GOD
Buddhism	It is a religion which does not include belief in a creator, deity or any eternal divine personal being.
Christadelphian	God is the creator of all things and the father of true believers; that he is a separate being from his son, Jesus Christ.
Christian Science	God is a pantheistic God – an all-embracing force or principle that lives in everything.
Hare Krishna	Krishna is the supreme God who oversees millions of demigods – who are seen as administrators of universal affairs. These demigods are needed to run creation.
Hinduism	Hindus actually only believe in one God, Brahman, the eternal origin who is the cause and foundation of all existence. The gods of the Hindu faith represent different forms of Brahman. Most Hindus have a personal god or goddess such as Shiva, Krishna or Lakshmi to whom they pray regularly.

NAME	WHAT THEY BELIEVE ABOUT GOD
Islam	One God (non-triune) that is Allah. He is supreme but not necessarily loving and merciful.
Jehovah's Witnesses	Non-triune and that God the Father alone is God. Jehovah is a poor anglicised version of God's name. It should be YHWH (pronounced 'Yahweh'). They believe that all true Christians should call God by this name.
Judaism	God is singular (non-triune) who not only created the universe but with whom every Jew can have an individual and personal relationship based on a covenant relationship.
Mormons	God the Father is the all-powerful and all-knowing supreme being who created the world. God the Father is a being called Elohim, who was once a man like present-day human beings, but who lived on another planet.

NAME	WHAT THEY BELIEVE ABOUT GOD
New Age	An impersonal force that is in everything that exists. There is no distinction between the creator and the creation.
Scientology	There is no specific dogma about God. Each member is allowed to come to their own conclusions about who or what God or the supreme being is.
Sikhism	There is only one God. Sikhs may also be called panentheistic, meaning that they believe God is present in creation. God is not the universe but is the life within it that drives it.
Spiritualism	An impersonal divine power and everything is within this power. This power can be destructive or constructive, light or dark, and therefore can be used for good and evil.

NAME	WHAT THEY BELIEVE ABOUT GOD
Wicca/Paganism	'God' or 'the divinity' could be male or female but most favour female. There may be many different expressions of goddesses or gods including Nature and Earth. All life is a manifestation of divinity.

I wonder what groups you are aware of or have interacted with? I wonder what groups you know about near to where you live? I wonder what groups you know about near to where your church is? Here's a useful exercise: google the different groups in this table so you can find out who is around. When you identify this you could chose to google those faiths and discover some of their back stories – again get to know these faiths so that when you engage with their followers, you are more prepared. Why not start to pray that God would bring you across their path so that you can develop a relationship with them, leading to dialogue.

As you have just looked at the table you may discover where you need to do some work. Where do you need to do some research to get a bit more of a grasp? I wouldn't necessarily read up on all the groups in the tables but rather consider who is around you or even who you think you might be most likely to have contact with and then put the work into those. For me it would be Jehovah's Witnesses and Muslims so I try to keep up to speed with those.

Whilst there are lots of similarities between Christianity and all the other faiths, there are lots of differences too. These are major differences to say the least. Whilst many of the cults and religions may say that they believe the same as us (in certain bits), they do so only in terms of the phrase and certainly not in terms of the theology. This can sometimes throw us. If we say, for example, to one group that we believe that Jesus is the Son of God, you may well find they agree. This, however, is not a statement of deity from their perspective whereas it is from a biblical perspective. A good thing to do when in discussion if they mention a particular phrase, such as the Son of God, is to ask the person what they understand or believe by that phrase.

Some would even talk of the Bible in really positive ways and yet the authority of the Bible would be denied as final. For example, Jehovah's Witnesses have their own 'translation' of the Bible whereas Mormons have their own Holy Book known as the Book of Mormon. Again, it's not my intention to go into these in great detail but simply to make you aware of the areas of difference. When you decide what the main groups you come into contact with are, you can then do further research and I would certainly encourage you to learn what the particular group believes.

In the next chapter I want to give you what I consider to be a generally good approach with all the faiths – that being the ability to show that Jesus was who he said he was and not what the particular person you are talking to has been told he or she should believe Jesus was. Along with this, another thing that makes Christianity different from any other religion or faith is that the founder not only died but came back to life – that is the game changer. Paul remarks on this in 1 Corinthians 15:14: 'And if Christ has not been raised, our preaching is useless and so is your faith.'

So, as you can see, they deny that Jesus was God. It would also be contested that Jesus never actually claimed to be God. We will pick this up in the next chapter but for now enjoy Tony Brown's story.

From Jehovah's Witness to Christ

TONY'S STORY

I had never really thought about God's existence. I was an ordinary lad from a council estate in Bradford just doing life. I had a good family, a job and a girlfriend; questions about why we are here or if there was an afterlife rarely entered my head, but that was about to change.

I was woken in the early hours of the morning by a banging on our front door. I could hear my sister's trembling voice shouting, 'She's gone!'

The death of my mother was sudden and unexpected. This was the first time I had suffered the loss of someone close to me. I was twenty-one years old. For the first time in my life, I had cause to consider life and death. 'Where has my mother gone?' 'Will I see her again?' My search began.

Having not been brought up in a religious home, I was not sure where to find the answers to my questions. I read a few books about the afterlife but I wasn't convinced. Then one day, my sister invited me to her house to meet some people she said could help me.

As the door opened, I saw a smartly dressed man and woman. They were very smiley and friendly. My sister invited them in and introduced me to them. They were Jehovah's Witnesses.

I began to fire all my questions at them and they, very calmly, opened their Bible and answered each one. I was hooked. I agreed to have a Bible study with them as soon as possible.

It didn't take long for me to begin to think like, sound like and look like a Jehovah's Witness. I quickly learned what the Bible said about a whole range of things and I was eager to share with my family, work colleagues and anyone who'd listen. The JWs became my new family.

One thing I believed wholeheartedly was that if I wanted to see my mother again, I needed to be a faithful witness of Jehovah. This meant attending all the meetings, staying away from worldly influences and, most importantly, knocking on people's doors. Although my family and friends didn't 'get it' I was convinced I had found the truth, so I spent most of the next four years involved with this group.

I began a new job and had heard that one of my colleagues was a Christian. This filled me with excitement. It became my mission to convert him to my way of thinking – after all, I had the truth.

David was an ordinary family man who frustrated the life out of me. He was unable to answer my questions, and I could tie him in knots with my 'proof-texts' proving that Jesus wasn't God. In my thinking, David hadn't got a clue about what the Bible taught, but then how could he? Only Jehovah's Witnesses truly understood the Bible.

Though unable to answer my objections (at least to my Jehovah's Witness satisfaction) I liked David. He had an attractive peaceful spirit about him. He always remained calm, whilst I often got worked up. On more than one occasion he invited me to his church, but Jehovah's Witnesses don't go to the false churches of Christendom.

David changed tack and invited me to have a meal with his family. Whilst there, I met some other Christians he'd invited. I wasn't happy, especially when one of them began to pray, and so after the meal I asked to leave. Although annoyed that David had invited others along, God was beginning to do a work in my life.

Not long after this, I asked David a question about something we had been learning about at the Kingdom Hall. His answer made more sense than what I had been taught. This was the first chink of light. Unbeknown to me at the time, the Holy Spirit was beginning to work in my life.

After some time, David invited me to a meeting at Bradford University. I reasoned that because it was not in a church I could go along. It was there that I heard the real gospel for the first time. That Jesus had died for me.

That I couldn't earn salvation but that it was a free gift. I was in tears, but also fearful.

I left the meeting a little confused and when I got home I looked up at the stars in the sky and prayed, 'God, please speak to me, please show me what is true.' When I woke the next day, I was full of a peace and a joy that I had never known. I felt like a great weight had been lifted from me. I called David who told me that I had been born-again. The very next day I walked into David's church to be greeted by a congregation that knew my name and had been praying for me for six months.

I had left the Jehovah's Witnesses and become the Jesus witness the Bible tells us we should be. Jesus said:

> *But you will receive power when the Holy Spirit comes on you; and you will be my witnesses in Jerusalem, and in all Judea and Samaria, and to the ends of the earth.* (Acts 1:8)

4

On this rock

Matthew 16:13-20 says, 'When Jesus came to the region of Caesarea Philippi, he asked his disciples, "Who do people say the Son of Man is?" They replied, "Some say John the Baptist; others say Elijah; and still others, Jeremiah or one of the prophets." "But what about you?" he asked. "Who do you say I am?" Simon Peter answered, "You are the Messiah, the Son of the living God." Jesus replied, "Blessed are you, Simon son of Jonah, for this was not revealed to you by flesh and blood, but by my Father in heaven. And I tell you that you are Peter, and on this rock I will build my church, and the gates of Hades will not overcome it."'

The church was built on the truth statement when Peter understood that Jesus was the Christ. It therefore comes as no surprise that denying who Jesus is forms the basis of other faiths, religions and cults. Paul goes on to tell us in 1 Corinthians 15:17, 'And if Christ has not been raised, your faith is futile; you are still in your sins.' It's an obvious statement but I'll make it anyway! These verses are linked theologically! Jesus' death brought forgiveness of sin and his resurrection brings guaranteed new life for those who believe. I believe spiritually that these are the main points we should chat about when sharing our faith with other faiths. They also form part of the gospel and it is the gospel that saves people, whoever they are.

Firstly, Jesus asked Peter who the people thought Jesus was but then Jesus focused in on Peter. For many people they have made up their mind by what others say about him rather than what they think about him. This is definitely true of those people in religions, faiths and cults. They define Jesus by what they have been told and I believe it's our opportunity to point them to who Jesus said he was and that it all makes sense. So what have they been told about who Jesus is?

NAME	WHAT THEY BELIEVE ABOUT JESUS
Buddhism	No belief in divine messenger, no need for a personal saviour. Just a man who did good.
Christadelphian	No pre-existence. His birth was his beginning. He was not called Christ until his baptism.
Christian Science	Not God, but son of God. He presented the Christ idea to the whole world same as New Age cosmic Christ. Jesus didn't actually die.
Hare Krishna	A directly empowered representative of Krishna who brought the message of a good way of life to his generation.
Hinduism	He is not unique but is recognised along with others as a holy man. He is not the expression of God in living form.
Islam	Held in high regard but just a prophet – the only prophet not to have sinned. Qur'an calls him Messiah. Mohammed was the highest prophet.

NAME	WHAT THEY BELIEVE ABOUT JESUS
Jehovah's Witnesses	First created being of Jehovah. Jesus then created everything else. He is a lesser God also called Michael the Archangel.
Judaism	Jesus was not the Messiah. Some believe him a false prophet, some a great teacher and some a false messiah.
Mormons	Title 'Son of God' accepted but a man like any other. He was married and had children. His death was not sufficient for forgiveness.
New Age	One of the religious leaders who manifested the Christ spirit. Not God and not unique.
Scientology	A special man with good teachings but he would still need Scientology. Jesus did not reach the highest level of Scientology which is 'truth revealed'.

NAME	WHAT THEY BELIEVE ABOUT JESUS
Sikhism	Sikhs do not believe that Jesus is God because Sikhism teaches that God is neither born nor dead. Jesus was born and lived a human life, therefore he cannot be God. He is respected.
Spiritualism	No pre-existence. His birth was his beginning. He was not called Christ until his baptism.
Wicca/Paganism	Some accept him as a magician, some would dismiss any belief in him. Jesus is not Son of God.

I really believe that our ability to build a good apologetic for the person of Jesus will stand us in good stead for sharing our faith with all faiths. Not only is it a good starting place for sharing with all faiths, it's also a vital ingredient even if we get into understanding one specific faith that we dialogue with.

We need to firmly establish these truths in the hearts of the people we are chatting to. To enable us to do this we need to understand what the different groups around us believe about Jesus. I have summed these up in the table – it would be useful to familiarise yourself with them.

Jesus claims to be God

It's often been said that Jesus (and the Bible) never claimed he was God. Well here are some verses to learn that help us to see that what people say is incorrect.

John 10:33: '"We [the Jews] are not stoning you for any good work," they replied, "but for blasphemy, because you, a mere man, claim to be God."'

What was the basis of this? Jesus made some pretty major claims in the previous few chapters and the Jews, who were fiercely monotheistic (believed in one God), knew that Jesus was claiming to be God. So Jesus claimed to be God. It was quite clear to many that Jesus was claiming to be God!

John 20:28: 'Thomas said to him, "My Lord and my God!"' Here Thomas acknowledges Jesus as God.

God claims Jesus is God! Hebrews 1:6 says, 'And again, when God brings his firstborn into the world, he says, "Let all God's angels worship him."' So we see from this verse that this is God speaking. Then in Hebrews 1:8 it says, 'But about the Son he says, "Your throne, O God, will last for ever and ever."' Here we can see that God calls Jesus God.

There are many more verses you can use but again, for the sake of keeping this booklet as a guide, we have looked at just a few. Let me encourage you to read some more.

It's worth noting that there is much reference about Jesus outside the Bible. Josephus, the great Jewish historian who wrote the history of the Jewish nation in about AD 90, tells us, 'At this time there was a wise man who was called Jesus. And his conduct was good and he was known to be virtuous. And many people from among the Jews and from other nations became his disciples. Pilate condemned him to be crucified and to die. And those who had become his disciples did not abandon his discipleship. They reported that he had appeared to them and that three days after his crucifixion he was alive.'

Tacitus, the great Roman historian, wrote in about AD 115 concerning the great fire of Rome and Nero's attempt to fasten the blame on the Christians. He says, 'Christus, from whom they take their name, had been executed by sentence of the procurator Pontius Pilate when Tiberius was governor.'

As I mentioned, the identity of Christ being the truth that the Christian faith is based on, it seems right to discuss this with people. Whilst there are difficulties with various parts of the Jesus story (e.g. the virgin birth), it is both my belief and my experience that the key issue is with the deity of Christ, that being his identity. It is therefore important to work on how we can show that Jesus was who he said he was. His death and resurrection are also what people struggle with and so we will look at this also.

When sharing your faith with other faiths the major problem is not whether Jesus existed but rather who he was. Most allow Jesus some place within their beliefs but only by relegating him to a mere man (albeit one of good moral standing), or at best a prophet. I find the best approach is to see whether we have the luxury of attributing this to Jesus. The great thing is we do have a slightly different starting point as these groups essentially recognise they've had to say something about him. In doing this he is broadly accepted as a great moral teacher of some sort. This, however, doesn't really work and so we will see the inconsistency and illogic of this as we reason in this next section.

The life of Jesus

When looking at the life of Jesus we're faced with two choices: Jesus' claims were true or they weren't. Let's say his claims weren't true. This also leaves us with two choices: he knew his claims were false or he didn't know his claims were false. If Jesus knew his claims were false then he was a liar. If he was a liar, then he was also a hypocrite because he spoke against all deceit. In fact it's far worse than that; he was the worst of all deceivers because he instructed others to entrust their eternity and future to him. He was also the biggest fool that ever walked the face of the earth because his claims forced his brutal punishment where he was nailed to a cross to die.

If Jesus actually thought he was God but in reality wasn't, we cannot, in fairness, call him a liar. All this was taking place in a fiercely monotheistic (one God) culture and here we have Jesus telling others he was God, he could forgive sins, he was the only way to heaven and to trust him with your future. The only conclusion we can draw from this explanation is that he was an absolute lunatic and a danger to human kind.

Was this the kind of person Jesus was? The only way to find out is to see if the life of Jesus is that of a lunatic or indeed a liar. This brings us on to the only other choice, which I mentioned at the beginning of this section – that his claims were true. If his claims are true then that challenges what other faiths believe about him!

So then, what did Jesus do? Well, he healed people of many diseases, he raised people from the dead, he led a faultless life, he confounded religious leaders (even when he was young), he spoke like no other person (others said this of him). He was a chief rabbi (a respected position), thousands flocked to see him (sometimes they went on ahead). He brought release to demonic lunatics (you don't hear of a lunatic freeing another lunatic).

Can we honestly look at this man and say anything other than his claims were true and that he was who he said he was? Not a liar, not a lunatic, but the Lord of heaven and earth.

Rousseau was a French man who was an opponent of Christianity. He said, 'If the life and death of Socrates are those of a philosopher, the life and death of Jesus are those of God.'

Jesus was God, he became a man, he lived a perfect life, he's the only Saviour of the world, he's the King of kings. Both Christian and non-Christian historians declare that a man named Jesus lived, was sentenced to death and that three days later his body was not in the tomb.

The death of Jesus

Just a note here that we covered this in chapter 2 when I talked about sharing the gospel. As a reminder I use this story to help illustrate.

> Imagine, if you will, that you are out walking on a dark night and you fall down a very deep pothole breaking your arms and legs – you are unable to move. To make things worse the water level is rising, giving you only a short time before you will be totally submerged. You start to shout for help as you are totally unable to do anything to get yourself out.

> Someone walks along and hears your shouts. They look down and say, 'I can see you are in trouble and unable to get out so what you need to do is . . .' They begin to tell you lots of stuff that all depends on you getting yourself out. That person then walks away. Your shouts continue until another person comes by and says, 'I can see you are in trouble so you need to enter into a state of inner peace and deny and ignore the trouble you are in.' They then continue on their way.

I use this to illustrate the fact that there is nothing we can do to get ourselves out of the mess we are in. There's nothing we can do to forget or ignore the reality or escape it. What we need is someone who will rescue us.

At this point, as you're shouting, another person walks by, looks down the pothole and says, 'I can see you are in trouble and that there is nothing you can do so I will come down and get you out myself.' That's the kind of help you want! I talk about how the mess we are in is a result of our wrongdoing and only Jesus can rescue us.

There are a number of Bible verses you can use but, as I said in chapter 2, I love John 14:6: 'Jesus answered, "I am the way and the truth and the life. No one comes to the Father except through me."' It leads us to consider the person of Jesus and not just what he did, which is so important.

In the following table I will show you what the different groups believe about salvation. This will help you choose your words and scriptures to help you talk about the salvation found in Jesus with understanding of where they are at so you can tailor your approach.

NAME	WHAT THEY BELIEVE ABOUT HOW WE CAN BE SAVED
Buddhism	Viewed as an escape from the continual cycle of rebirth (reincarnation). To get to this point (Nirvana), there has to be the accomplishment of so many good works that the law of fate that adds up the good and bad things we do in this life (karma) allows them to be released.
Christadelphian	Christ's death not enough to save us from the penalty of our sins; good works are also needed although some say that grace is enough, but when investigated salvation can only be kept by fulfilling the biblical law.
Christian Science	A person is saved when they are set free from the illusion of believing in this unreal world of matter and sinfulness. This 'mind over matter' is reached by studying, accepting and believing what Eddy wrote.

NAME	WHAT THEY BELIEVE ABOUT HOW WE CAN BE SAVED
Hare Krishna	Salvation is seen as being released from the reincarnation cycle which happens by coming to Krishna consciousness. This is done by cultivating knowledge by carefully reading Srila Prabhupada's books and asking questions of other devotees who can give enlightened answers.
Hinduism	Similar to Buddhism, Hinduism is seeking release from the continual cycle of rebirth but it is achieved by ritual prayers and following a sacred code of conduct. The three main paths of devotion, action and knowledge can lead to this release.
Islam	It can only be achieved by striving and a man's own effort. The four main ways to achieve this are: pre-destination by Allah, martyrdom, pilgrimage to Mecca and animal sacrifice, and by good works.

NAME	WHAT THEY BELIEVE ABOUT HOW WE CAN BE SAVED
Jehovah's Witnesses	Two-tier salvation. Only 144,000 will rule with Jesus in heaven and the rest will live in paradise on earth after the Battle of Armageddon. Becoming a member of the Watchtower Society (this is the organisation) is the key to salvation rather than a personal relationship with Jesus.
Judaism	Prayer, repentance, obedience to Jewish religious law and good works are required. Some believe salvation is the improvement of society. This is since the temple was destroyed in AD 70 when Judaism became more of a religion of the temple and so didn't need sacrifices.

NAME	WHAT THEY BELIEVE ABOUT HOW WE CAN BE SAVED
Mormons	Different levels of salvation but full salvation is in the highest of three heavens which is for those who have fulfilled every law and ordinance of Mormonism (including not drinking caffeine drinks). It's said to be by God's grace but this only happens when you have done everything (the good works) you need to do.
New Age	A release from the earthly life into some form of eternal reward. New Agers have different beliefs about how this happens but basically the law of karma – i.e. good deeds weighed against bad deeds – determines what happens (reincarnation) in the next life. When this balances you are released from the cycle of reincarnation.

NAME	WHAT THEY BELIEVE ABOUT HOW WE CAN BE SAVED
Scientology	By purchasing counselling courses from Scientologists and undertaking their auditing, 'engrams' can be removed and an individual can enter a clear state which releases them from the cycle of rebirth. An 'engram' is received when an individual has an emotional experience in this or a previous life, meaning they are in a 'preclear' state.
Sikhism	In order to attain salvation one must live an honest life and meditate on God. Sikhism shows the way to attain salvation and become one with God.
Spiritualism	Based on the beliefs of karma and reincarnation, an individual has many lives until their good deeds finally balance out their bad deeds. When this happens they have reached enlightenment and can be released from this earthly body.

NAME	WHAT THEY BELIEVE ABOUT HOW WE CAN BE SAVED
Wicca/Paganism	Wherever the individual believes they are going (there are many beliefs in this grouping about life after death), they will get there by doing good works or progressing through forms of karma and reincarnation.

The resurrection of Jesus

There have been many attempts to explain away the resurrection – not surprising really – our faith is in vain if it is proved wrong. Frank Morison, a lawyer, tried to write a book to disprove the resurrection. During his investigations he realised the resurrection happened. He wrote a book called *Who Moved the Stone?* The first chapter is called 'The Book that Refused to be Written'. In it he tells his testimony of how he became a Christian. Some of the key objections to Jesus' resurrection are briefly dealt with here.

FRAUD: A Roman guard was placed around the tomb at the request of the Jews in case anything happened. The tomb was made secure and watched over. The guard then fell asleep and the disciples came up by night and stole the body. They then made up a story that Jesus had risen from the dead and so the biggest hoax of all time was perpetrated. A Roman guard was a sixteen-man security unit, with each member highly trained. If one man failed in his duty, all sixteen were executed. To coin a phrase, they would have 'kept an eye on each other'.

If the disciples stole the body, what was the point of leaving the linen cloth Jesus was wrapped in? They would have made a quicker departure if they had left the grave clothes on Jesus.

How did the guards not hear them move the three-tonne stone? Nearly every one of the early disciples died for their faith. Would you die for something you didn't sincerely believe was true?

Jesus' disciples were depressed and disheartened. They thought Jesus was dead and buried. Yet something happened that day that suddenly made them bold, turning them into people who told everybody that Jesus had risen. We still have Christians around today as a result of the 'truth' of Jesus' resurrection. What do these disciples and Christians today have in common?

SWOON: Jesus didn't really die! What actually happened is Jesus fainted with exhaustion on the cross. In the coolness of the tomb he revived then quietly pushed back the stone (three tonnes) that covered the entrance to the tomb, yet didn't disturb the Roman guard in doing so. When he was seen by his disciples they jumped to the wrong conclusion that he had risen from the dead. Let's examine this.

Once again, the Roman soldiers knew their job well. It would have meant death if they made a mistake. Pilate wouldn't have given permission for Joseph to bury Jesus if he wasn't dead. Put yourself in this position.

A crown of thorns that would pierce your skull is pushed into your head. Thirty-nine lashes of the whip (forty would result in death). Your flesh would be hanging off your back. It would be like a ploughed field. The walk to the crucifixion site with the cross on your back was enough to kill the fittest. Your joints dislocated as the cross was set in place. You would be fighting for every breath as you began to suffocate. Finally, as the spear was thrust into your side, blood and water flowed. This was due to acute dilation of the stomach. If you weren't dead already you would be now. You were left without food or water for three days. Surely, without medical attention serious infection would set in as you lay in the tomb.

Okay, let's say he really didn't die (highly improbable), he fainted and then he revived. Is it possible for this man, on the brink of death, to push away the stone? Not only that, but during the forty days and nights he was on the earth, he said to Thomas, who didn't believe, 'See the nails prints in my hand' – surely the fact that Jesus had to point out the nail prints in his hands shows that the rest of his body was totally healed. If it wasn't, why did he need to say what he did. Everybody would have seen his injuries. Only by a miracle would they have healed. Jesus didn't faint and then revive. God performed a miracle by raising Jesus from the dead and restoring his health.

Mary, Jesus' mum, recognised him on the cross and believed him. Will you? Disciples recognised the empty tomb and sought to find him. Will you? They recognised the risen Jesus and followed him. Will you?

DELUSION: The disciples expected Jesus to rise again so much that eventually they hallucinated and saw Jesus. So actually the whole resurrection was an hallucination by all five hundred people who saw it. It was all in the mind! The truth is, however, that the whole crucifixion took the disciples by surprise. They were frightened because Jesus, their leader, was gone. They hid for fear of death. They certainly didn't expect Jesus to rise again. Delusions can only happen when people expect something so much that they start to believe it. Delusions are individualistic. It is highly unlikely that two will have the same one at the same time. Can five hundred have the same delusion? No. Delusions usually increase in intensity and occur over a long period of time. They don't suddenly stop after forty days. Okay, let's say that they did hallucinate! That would mean Jesus was still in the tomb. If the Jews were so afraid of Jesus rising again from the dead, why didn't they just show the body of Jesus still in the tomb?

MIRACLE: Jesus was on the cross. He gave up his ghost. The centurion said Jesus was the Son of God. He died. He was taken down from the cross and put in a tomb. Three days later he wasn't there. Over the next forty days about five hundred people, from all walks of life, saw him and their lives were radically changed. They never found a 'dead Jesus' in the tomb and the impact of that is still being felt today. Let's build on this rock – it's a good way forward.

If Jesus rose again from the dead then that, along with him being God, also challenges what the different faiths and cults believe. It not only means that our faith is not in vain; it also means that their faith is.

In the following table I will show you what the different groups believe about death. This will help you choose your words and scriptures to talk about new life found in Jesus with understanding of where they are at so you can tailor your approach.

NAME	WHAT THEY BELIEVE ABOUT DEATH
Buddhism	The dead are reborn according to their karma into one of several realms until the cycle is ended when they reach Nirvana.
Christadelphian	We will live for all eternity on earth. They don't believe that we will go to heaven; there is no hell. Those who don't make it to salvation on earth are simply annihilated.
Christian Science	Hell is a state of mind and so once released from it, it no longer exists. Heaven is the place of reality in another dimension which is accessed by the acceptance of the divine Principle of Christian Science.
Hare Krishna	Unless an individual is fully Krishna conscious, they have to accept a body in the next life according to their state of consciousness. Once full Krishna consciousness is achieved, the next time they die they do not accept another material body but rather return home, back to Krishna.

NAME	WHAT THEY BELIEVE ABOUT DEATH
Hinduism	Only the body dies but the spirit (or soul) lives on. It comes again in many different bodies until the final iteration from the rebirth cycle is achieved.
Islam	If they are good enough, a Muslim goes to heaven. This is seen as a physical resurrection. If they aren't good enough they go to hell, which is also physical (i.e. flames, torment).
Jehovah's Witnesses	At death a person goes out of existence and only remains a memory in the mind of God. After Armageddon all who are worthy will be resurrected back to the earth. They will be given a second chance at salvation during Christ's one-hundred-year reign.

NAME	WHAT THEY BELIEVE ABOUT DEATH
Judaism	There will be a resurrection and a judgment as the soul is immortal. Other than this commonality, Judaism varies in terms of what happens next e.g. about what heaven is like and whether there is a hell. Most do believe that the righteous of all nations do have a share in the world to come.
Mormons	There are three kingdoms in the afterlife: Celestial, Terrestrial and Telestial. For men who reach the highest level (Celestial) they can become gods and live on their own planet with their goddess wives. The second level (Terrestrial) is for all 'good people' – a lesser salvation. The third (Telestial) is for wicked people.

NAME	WHAT THEY BELIEVE ABOUT DEATH
New Age	Death simply brings another lifetime until the individual is released from further reincarnations because the karma balances (good deeds weighed against bad deeds). Then they can move onto their reward.
Scientology	There are many rebirths until Scientology has brought the individual to the ultimate state of 'clear'. When this happens they can move to a state of 'heaven' when they next die as they are now freed from rebirth.
Sikhism	Death is only physical and the soul lives on through reincarnation. Through a long series of reincarnations, possibly through up to 8,400,000 forms of life, they will be purified and be able to return to Waheguru (the word used in Sikhism to refer to God).

NAME	WHAT THEY BELIEVE ABOUT DEATH
Spiritualism	Some Spiritists believe in a hell but you can get out of it and up through the levels of reward. Some believe in a type of heavenly existence. For most the understanding is that the afterlife is just a fourth dimension.
Wicca/Paganism	Hell and punishment do not exist. Most believe that Christians have invented hell and the devil. There is a broad range of belief in this area, from annihilation to the Divinity again.

I hope you have found the information as helpful as I do when sharing my faith with followers of other faiths. I'm not promising mass conversion but I am promising meaningful conversations with people from other faiths. That is a very good starting point.

But before you go, one last testimony from Hani Shadad.

From Islam to Christ
HANI'S STORY

I thought that I knew who God was!

I thought things were good yet I tried not to remember my past, where I came from and how I arrived here. I grew up in a loving but dysfunctional family. I was looked after and yet I was lonely.

Islam played a big part of my life both at home and in school, as well as among friendships! Life wasn't easy but I always found a way to survive. I found a way to travel and study and work and to stay safe in the midst of air strikes, civil wars and earthquakes.

I became a refugee at a very young age, finding myself travelling from one continent to another. It meant I lost friends as well as made new ones. The more I travelled, the faster I became detached from people and also detached from myself. I was just doing what other people were doing comfortably, I guess, coasting to nowhere.

I became religious, trying to get the attention of God as I knew him. I started to pray five times a day, do my Friday ritual. My wife came from a Catholic background but she was struggling with her spirituality at the time. We had two weddings – one in a mosque and the second in the church. It was very expensive but we wanted to please our families. I used to work long hours and even extra hours at nights, at the weekends. That meant no church for her as she had to look after our children. I hadn't realised I was choking her spiritually at the time.

My life took twist after twist but I was comfortable with less. One night, whilst I was asleep, I saw a man in my dream and I heard a voice giving me a message. I had never met the man before. When I woke up, I thought the dream and the man with the message were weird. But then I met that man in real life, the very first thing that morning! I could not even say hi to him, I literally walked off when he tried to shake my hand. But for some reason I couldn't rest that day until I asked a friend. Later that day the friend took me back to see the man and introduced me to him. I had to tell him something – about the dream and the message. He started to cry, and I was crying too.

The following night I had another dream with a different man but the same voice. This time the voice asked me a question instead of giving me a message. He asked me, 'Do you know who this person is?' I said, 'No.' He said to me, 'This is Jesus!'

As a Muslim those dreams started to confuse me, maybe provoked something within me. I asked myself 'Why me?' 'What does he want for me?' 'Do any Muslims see

Jesus in their dreams?' I thought I was going crazy. I was in a searching mood, reading books, searching on the internet, checking YouTube, reading the Bible and the Qur'an. Honestly, I didn't get anything mentally or spiritually out of my research. Then I decided to stop reading and listening and I just went for a walk. I talked with whoever it was up there. It became a friendship of daily walk and talk.

Three years down the road I came to an understanding that if I became a Christian my life was finished. I left myself open to doubts and fear and I wanted to know that I am not just following a dream. I had three questions: Is God going to be with me and protect me? Who is God? What for?

In the midst of all that was happening, my wife joined a new church and my younger son was going with her. My son invited me to the Christmas celebration. That morning I heard about the Alpha course for the first time. By this point I had one lingering question that I needed an answer to: Why didn't Jesus ask me to become a Christian? In that Alpha course I found the answer out for myself.

I am now a Christian, fully devoted to Jesus. I love telling people about him. I go on missions with Elim International Missions and I love to tell my story. I was a Muslim who didn't really know where he was going in life, and now I am a Christian who is fully purposed.

Acknowledgements

Special thanks to Tony Brown and Reachout Trust who have supplied Sandy's and Marisa's stories as well as Tony's own. Also special thanks to Hani for supplying his story.

Thanks again to Reachout Trust who supplied much material when I first started out sharing my faith with Jehovah's Witnesses and Mormons. You got me going and, actually, it was those early stages that inspired me to pull together the very first version of this book.

Thanks again to Ashdown Creative for working their design skills on my work.

Thanks to Louise Stenhouse who once again helped me make sense by proofing and editing the copy.

Thanks to Chris Powell and Verité CM Ltd for your continued work getting my books published.

VISIT
www.revmarkgreenwood.com
where you will find a shop full of really helpful resources.

Notes

Notes

_____

_____

_____

_____

_____

_____

_____

_____

_____

_____

_____

_____

_____

_____

Notes

_____

_____

_____

_____

_____

_____

_____

_____

_____

_____

_____

_____

_____

Notes

_____

_____

_____

_____

_____

_____

_____

_____

_____

_____

_____

_____

_____

_____

Notes